ADVENT WORSHIP GUIDE

This book was written and assembled by LifePoint Church. The material and format have been influenced by the Book of Common Prayer (2019), as well as historic Christian prayers found in the Pocket Book of Prayers, published by Barnes and Noble as well as Be Thou My Vision: A Liturgy for Daily Worship by Jonathan Gibson, published by Crossway. Some material is taken directly from these sources.

This book was printed at Ingram Books in LaVergne, TN.

For more information, please contact LifePoint Church.
Website: lifepointchurch.org
Phone: (615) 459-3311

Table of Contents

How To Use This Book

The word Advent means "arrival." The Advent season is a dedicated time of the year where the people of God remember the arrival of the Savior, Jesus Christ, to the world. For thousands of years, God's people waited with eager longing and expectation for the One who would come to undo sin's curse. They groaned for the Savior who would come and right all that sin made wrong. They cried out for the Deliverer who would save them from the sting of death.

Scan to watch a vi explaining how to the book.

Two thousand years ago in a little town called Bethlehem, that person appeared. He did not arrive to shouts of victory. He did not fly in on a chariot of fire. He came quietly, born to an ordinary mother and father. But this was no ordinary child, for He was God wrapped up in a few pounds of human flesh. The Promised Savior was God, Himself; come to put on human skin, live a human life, stretch out His human arms, and die a human death so that all humanity may turn to Him to be saved.

This season, and this worship guide, is meant to aid you as you remember, rejoice, and rest in the sweetness of the Savior's advent.

This guide is made up of two parts:
1. **Daily Advent Meditations**
2. **Weekly Worship Guides**

Daily Advent Meditations

The Daily Advent Meditations span 29 days, and are meant to be read during personal devotions in addition to your existing Bible reading plan. You should begin this on Sunday, November 27, the first day of Advent. Each reading is fewer than 20 verses, so please do not rush through them. Rather, read them slowly. Read them multiple times and deeply ponder what the words say considering what the Holy Spirit would show you through them. Allow yourself to be amazed by the wonder of the incarnation of the Lord Jesus Chirst, the Savior of the world.

Weekly Advent Worship Guide

The Weekly Worship Guide is meant to be done weekly in a group. This may be family, friends, neighbors, or a Life Group. In this guide you will find readings, prayers, songs, and activities meant to focus your hearts on the incarnation of the Lord Jesus. Choose one night a week that you know will work for everyone, and set aside 15-20 minutes to work through the guide together. In the midst of busy lives and hectic holiday schedules, it is important that we take time to recenter our hearts on the Lord Jesus.

Certain sections of the guide are assigned to the **Leader.** For a group doing this together, this will be the group leader or another suitable member. For families, this will typically be a Christian father who will be responsible for leading the family through the worship guide. However, if there is no Christian father in the home, the mother or another suitable member should serve as the Leader. The sections assigned to the Group will be those members other than the Leader.

Take your time as your family/group walks through this weekly time of worship. This is meant to be a reflective time with family and friends. Follow the directions found in the small font. This will lead you through the worship guide.

Advent Wreath Preparation

During weekly Family/Group worship, you will light a candle on your Advent wreath. If you do not have one, be sure to gather the materials to make one before you start, or assemble the wreath during the first weekly worship time. You will need to clear a space for the Advent candles, preferably in a place that is visible during your normal movements throughout the home. You will need five candles (three purple, one pink, and one white). The three purple candles represent Hope, Peace, and Joy; the pink candle represents Love; and the white candle represents Christ. You may also gather other materials with which to decorate your Advent wreath, as well as the place where you put it.

Families with Young Children

Families with young children are encouraged to do the following:

- **Lighting of the Advent Candle**
- **Family Scripture Reading**
- **Singing of a Hymn**
- **Closing Prayer**
- **Activities for Families with Young Children**

For ease of use, the following symbol is placed next to the sections families should complete.

The rest of the guide can be completed with the adults and older children at another time, perhaps after the younger children have gone to bed.

Daily Advent Meditations

Each day of Advent, set aside time to personally meditate on the passages of Scripture below. Read them slowly. Read them multiple times. Deeply ponder what the words say, and consider what the Holy Spirit shows you through them.

Before you begin reading, pray this:

Open my eyes, O Lord, that I may behold wondrous things out of your Law.

— Psalm 119:18 —

November 27	Isaiah 8:22-9:7
November 28	Psalm 89:19-29
November 29	Isaiah 11:1-10
November 30	Psalm 2:1-12
December 1	Genesis 3:8-15
December 2	Psalm 118:19-29
December 3	Genesis 17:1-9
December 4	Psalm 45:1-9
December 5	Micah 5:1-6
December 6	Psalm 110:1-7
December 7	John 1:1-18
December 8	Matthew 1:1-17
December 9	Luke 1:1-17
December 10	Luke 1:18-25
December 11	Luke 1:26-38
December 12	Luke 1:39-45
December 13	Luke 1:46-56
December 14	Luke 1:57-66
December 15	Luke 1:67-80
December 16	Matthew 1:18-25
December 17	Luke 2:1-7
December 18	Luke 2:8-14
December 19	Luke 2:15-21
December 20	Matthew 2:1-12
December 21	Matthew 2:13-18
December 22	Matthew 2:19-23
December 23	Luke 2:22-32
December 24	Luke 2:33-40
December 25	Online Program

HOPE

WEEK 1

Opening Blessing

The Leader may begin by reading one or more of the following. Read slowly, and allow the words to guide your hearts as you begin your time of worship.

Glory to God in the highest, and on earth peace among those with whom he is pleased!

— Luke 2:14 —

"Hear, O Israel: The Lord our God, the Lord is one. You shall love the Lord your God with all your heart and with all your soul and with all your might. And these words that I command you today shall be on your heart.

— Deuteronomy 6:4-6 —

The people who walked in darkness
  have seen a great light;
those who dwelt in a land of deep darkness,
  on them has light shone.
You have multiplied the nation;
  you have increased its joy;
they rejoice before you
  as with joy at the harvest,
  as they are glad when they divide the spoil.

— Isaiah 9:2-3 —

Lighting the Advent Candle

The Leader will go to the Advent table and light the Hope candle, the first candle of the Advent wreath. After doing so, the Leader will join the Group and say:

LEADER: The things of this world are passing away.

GROUP: But God's Word remains forever.

LEADER: The world is full of despair.

GROUP: But God's people will not lose hope.

LEADER: Always be near us, Lord Jesus.

GROUP: We hope in You, always.

Preparation for Worship and Scripture Reading

The Leader says:

As we approach the throne of our Holy God, we must do so with open hearts. God teaches us that we are not to hide our sins from Him, but rather, we are to confess them freely so as to receive forgiveness and restoration by His grace. Our God is infinitely full of tenderness and love toward us. He never rejects us, despite our many failures. We will approach Him now to confess our sins and prepare our hearts.

The Group will remain silent for 30 seconds while each member privately confesses their sins to God.

The Leader will then read this assurance of forgiveness over the Group:

If we say we have no sin, we deceive ourselves, and the truth is not in us. If we confess our sins, He is faithful and just to forgive us our sins and to cleanse us from all unrighteousness.

— 1 John 1:8-9 —

The Leader will then prepare for the reading of Scripture by praying:

O, make your Word a swift Word,
passing from the ear to the heart,
from the heart to the lip and conversation;
that, as the rain returns not empty,
so neither may your Word,
but accomplish that for which it is given. Amen.

— George Herbert (1593)

The Leader will take a Bible and say to the Group:

God's Word is the truth. It is truer than true. It is the greatest treasure we have. In these pages, the Lord Jesus Christ is revealed to us. This home is built upon God's unfailing Word, and our lives are governed by all that He has commanded. Let us never forget this great gift.

The Group will then pray.

LEADER: Oh Lord, we thank You for Your Word.

GROUP: Open our eyes to see You.

LEADER: Father, bless us as we read it.

GROUP: That we may always obey You.

LEADER: Christ, purify us through it.

GROUP: That we may always honor You.

LEADER: Holy Spirit, help us to understand it.

GROUP: That we may always proclaim You.

LEADER: Praise the Lord.

ALL TOGETHER: The Lord's Name be praised.

The Reading of Scripture and Lessons

The Leader will then turn to Matthew 1:18-25. The passage may be read by the Leader or another Group member.

18Now the birth of Jesus Christ took place in this way. When his mother Mary had been betrothed to Joseph, before they came together she was found to be with child from the Holy Spirit. 19And her husband Joseph, being a just man and unwilling to put her to shame, resolved to divorce her quietly. 20But as he considered these things, behold, an angel of the Lord appeared to him in a dream, saying, "Joseph, son of David, do not fear to take Mary as your wife, for that which is conceived in her is from the Holy Spirit. 21She will bear a son, and you shall call his name Jesus, for he will save his people from their sins." 22All this took place to fulfill what the Lord had spoken by the prophet:

23"Behold, the virgin shall conceive and bear a son,
   and they shall call his name Immanuel"

(which means, God with us). 24When Joseph woke from sleep, he did as the angel of the Lord commanded him: he took his wife, 25but knew her not until she had given birth to a son. And he called his name Jesus.

— Matthew 1:18–25 —

At the end of the reading:

> LEADER: This is the Word of the Lord.

> GROUP: Thanks be to God.

The Leader will then say:

> Today we are reflecting on Jesus Christ, our Hope. Oftentimes, we can forget what great hope we have in Christ because there are so many things that try to take our hope away. What are some things that distract us from the hope we have in Christ?

The Group will give their answers.

The head of household will then say:

> It's important for us to remember that Christ is greater than the world. Because God the Father sent His Son, we can have confidence that He will work all things for our good and His glory. Scripture says that Jesus shall be called Immanuel, which means "God with us." This title reminds us that no matter the chaos we experience, no matter the pain we endure, and no matter the uncertainty of the future, Christ is always with us. And if God is with us, who can stand against us?

> Let us praise God for the hope we have in Christ.

Family/Group Scripture Reading

The Leader will then turn to Isaiah 9:1-7. This passage may be read by any member of the Group.

¹But there will be no gloom for her who was in anguish. In the former time he brought into contempt the land of Zebulun and the land of Naphtali, but in the latter time he has made glorious the way of the sea, the land beyond the Jordan, Galilee of the nations.

²The people who walked in darkness
   have seen a great light;
those who dwelt in a land of deep darkness,
   on them has light shone.
³You have multiplied the nation;
   you have increased its joy;
they rejoice before you
   as with joy at the harvest,
   as they are glad when they divide the spoil.
⁴For the yoke of his burden,
   and the staff for his shoulder,
   the rod of his oppressor,
   you have broken as on the day of Midian.
⁵For every boot of the tramping warrior in battle tumult
   and every garment rolled in blood
   will be burned as fuel for the fire.
⁶For to us a child is born,
   to us a son is given;
and the government shall be upon his shoulder,

The
PEOPLE
WHO WALKED
IN
DARKNESS
HAVE SEEN A
GREAT
LIGHT
—ISAIAH 9:2

and his name shall be called

Wonderful Counselor, Mighty God,

Everlasting Father, Prince of Peace.

7Of the increase of his government and of peace

there will be no end,

on the throne of David and over his kingdom,

to establish it and to uphold it

with justice and with righteousness

from this time forth and forevermore.

The zeal of the Lord of hosts will do this.

— Isaiah 9:1–7 —

LEADER: The grass withers, the flower fades, but the Word of God remains forever.

GROUP: Amen.

The Singing of a Hymn

In a posture of thankfulness and worship, the Group will then say or sing this hymn together:

O Come O Come Emmanuel

O Come, o come Emmanuel
And ransom captive Israel
That mourns in lonely exile here
Until the Son of God appear

Rejoice, rejoice!
Emmanuel shall come to thee, O Israel

O come, o come thou Lord of might
Who to Thy tribes on Sinai's height
In ancient times did give the law
In cloud, in majesty, and awe

O come Thou Day-spring, come and cheer
Our spirits by Thine advent here
Disperse the gloomy clouds of night
And death's dark shadow put to flight

If desired, the Group may sing the additional Hymn,
Come Thou Long Expected Jesus, located in the back of this book.

Scan to sing
hymn with
music and
video.

Closing Blessing

The Leader will then close with this prayer:

Almighty God, heavenly Father, we ask you to work in us by your Holy Spirit, so that we may rightly know you, and sanctify, glorify, and praise you in all your works, in which shine forth your omnipotence, wisdom, goodness, righteousness, mercy, and truth. Grant us also that we may so direct our whole life - thoughts, words and deeds - that your name is not blasphemed because of us, but honored and praised. Amen.
— Zacharias Ursinus (1534)

The Group will then say the Gloria Patri together:

Glory be to the Father, and to the Son, and to the Holy Spirit; as it was in the beginning, is now, and will be forever. Amen.

The Leader will then say:

May the God of hope fill you with all joy and peace in believing, so that by the power of the Holy Spirit you may abound in hope.
— Romans 15:13 —

Closing Prayer For Families with Young Children

Father, You are our only source of hope. You are everything that we need. Thank You for always providing for our Family. Help us to trust You with our every need that we have and to fully put our trust in You. Thank You for being the God of Hope. Amen

Activities For Families with Young Children

Activity 1:

Draw a picture of an anchor. Let the kids decorate the anchor. Hang the picture in a place where everyone in the Family can see it. Use the picture as an accountability tool when someone in the Family is living in expectation for something other than the hope of the Lord.

Activity 2:

Using paper or pieces of cardboard, create a "stepping stone" path from one side of your living room to the other. Add small challenges along the way, perhaps a chair to climb over or narrow "balance beam" made of masking tape. As you walk, talk about the obstacles we face in life: moving to a different school, making new friends, being sick. Now place a blindfold over your child's eyes. Explain that often we can't see how to get through the obstacles in our lives. Take your child's hand and guide him along each step of the path, explaining that we can face the challenges of life because we know that God is with us. Even if we can't always see where we're headed, our hope comes from knowing that God directs our steps.

Application:

Share the Hope of Christ by writing Christmas Cards sharing the Gospel with your teachers, classmates, co-workers and others. On Sunday, grab some Christmas Eve invite cards from your local campus to give out as you share the Hope of Christ. Encourage your students to take invite cards to school for friends and teachers.

PEACE

WEEK 2

Opening Blessing

The Leader may begin by reading one or more of the following. Read slowly, and allow the words to guide your hearts as you begin your time of worship.

Glory to God in the highest, and on earth peace among those with whom he is pleased!

— Luke 2:14 —

"Hear, O Israel: The Lord our God, the Lord is one. You shall love the Lord your God with all your heart and with all your soul and with all your might. And these words that I command you today shall be on your heart.

— Deuteronomy 6:4-6 —

The people who walked in darkness
   have seen a great light;
those who dwelt in a land of deep darkness,
   on them has light shone.
You have multiplied the nation;
   you have increased its joy;
they rejoice before you
   as with joy at the harvest,
     as they are glad when they divide the spoil.

— Isaiah 9:2-3 —

 Lighting the Advent Candle

The Leader will go to the Advent table and light the Peace candle, the second candle of the Advent wreath. After doing so, the Leader will join the Group and say:

LEADER: The things of this world are passing away.

GROUP: But God's Word remains forever.

LEADER: The world is full of pain.

GROUP: But God's people have everlasting peace.

LEADER: Have mercy on us, Lord Jesus.

GROUP: Be our Prince of Peace forever.

Preparation for Worship and Scripture Reading

The Leader says:

As we approach the throne of our Holy God, we must do so with open hearts. God teaches us that we are not to hide our sins from Him, but rather, we are to confess them freely so as to receive forgiveness and restoration by His grace. Our God is infinitely full of tenderness and love toward us. He never rejects us, despite our many failures. We will approach Him now to confess our sins and prepare our hearts.

The Group will remain silent for 30 seconds while each member privately confesses their sins to God.

While remaining in a posture of prayer, the Leader will read this assurance of forgiveness over the Group:

> In Him we have redemption through His blood, the forgiveness of our trespasses, according to the riches of His grace, which He lavished upon us, in all wisdom and insight making known to us the mystery of His will, according to His purpose, which He set forth in Christ as a plan for the fullness of time, to unite all things in Him, things in heaven and things on earth.
>
> — Ephesians 1:7-10 —

The Leader will then prepare for the reading of Scripture by praying:

> Blessed Lord, you have caused all Holy Scriptures to be written for our learning - grant us that we may in such a way hear them, read, mark, learn, and inwardly digest them; that by patience and comfort of your holy Word, we may embrace and ever hold fast the blessed hope of everlasting life, which you have given us in our Savior Jesus Christ. Amen.
>
> — Book of Common Prayer (1552)

The Leader will take a Bible and say to the Group:

God's Word is the truth. It is truer than true. It is the greatest treasure we have. In these pages, the Lord Jesus Christ is revealed to us. This home is built upon God's unfailing Word, and our lives are governed by all that He has commanded. Let us never forget this great gift.

The Group will then pray.

LEADER: Oh Lord, we thank You for Your Word.

GROUP: Open our eyes to see You.

LEADER: Father, bless us as we read it.

GROUP: That we may always obey You.

LEADER: Christ, purify us through it.

GROUP: That we may always honor You.

LEADER: Holy Spirit, help us to understand it.

GROUP: That we may always proclaim You.

LEADER: Praise the Lord.

ALL TOGETHER: The Lord's Name be praised.

The Reading of Scripture and Lessons

The Leader will then turn to Genesis 3:1-15. The passage may be read by the Leader or another Group member.

---

[1] Now the serpent was more crafty than any other beast of the field that the Lord God had made.

He said to the woman, "Did God actually say, 'You shall not eat of any tree in the garden'?" [2] And the woman said to the serpent, "We may eat of the fruit of the trees in the garden, [3] but God said, 'You shall not eat of the fruit of the tree that is in the midst of the garden, neither shall you touch it, lest you die.'" [4] But the serpent said to the woman, "You will not surely die. [5] For God knows that when you eat of it your eyes will be opened, and you will be like God, knowing good and evil." [6] So when the woman saw that the tree was good for food, and that it was a delight to the eyes, and that the tree was to be desired to make one wise, she took of its fruit and ate, and she also gave some to her husband who was with her, and he ate. [7] Then the eyes of both were opened, and they knew that they were naked. And they sewed fig leaves together and made themselves loincloths.

[8] And they heard the sound of the Lord God walking in the garden in the cool of the day, and the man and his wife hid themselves from the presence of the Lord God

among the trees of the garden. ⁹But the Lord God called to the man and said to him, "Where are you?" ¹⁰And he said, "I heard the sound of you in the garden, and I was afraid, because I was naked, and I hid myself." ¹¹He said, "Who told you that you were naked? Have you eaten of the tree of which I commanded you not to eat?" ¹²The man said, "The woman whom you gave to be with me, she gave me fruit of the tree, and I ate." ¹³Then the Lord God said to the woman, "What is this that you have done?" The woman said, "The serpent deceived me, and I ate."

¹⁴The Lord God said to the serpent, "Because you have done this, cursed are you above all livestock and above all beasts of the field; on your belly you shall go, and dust you shall eat all the days of your life. ¹⁵I will put enmity between you and the woman, and between your offspring and her offspring; he shall bruise your head, and you shall bruise his heel."

— Genesis 3:1-15 —

At the end of the reading:

LEADER: This is the Word of the Lord.

GROUP: Thanks be to God.

The Leader will then say:

Today we reflect on Jesus Christ, our Peace. Everywhere around us we see chaos and destruction. It appears there is no true peace on earth today. Because of our rebellion against God—from Adam and Eve's rebellion to our own—humanity has forsaken the peace of Christ for the chaos of sin. What are the ways this is most evident?

The Group will give their answers.

In the story we just read, we saw Adam and Eve rebel against God. But in the last verse, God promises to bring redemption to the world that sin corrupted. When Adam and Eve sinned, God didn't give them what they deserved. Instead, He promised that one day a Savior would come. One who would bring grace, forgiveness, and peace to the people of God. Jesus first brings peace between us and God, and through this, He also brings peace between us and others. No one can produce lasting and enduring peace like Jesus.

Let us praise God for the peace we have been given in Christ.

Family/Group Scripture Reading

The Leader will then turn to Isaiah 11:1-9. This passage may be read by any member of the Group.

> [1]There shall come forth a shoot from the stump of Jesse,
>   and a branch from his roots shall bear fruit.
> [2]And the Spirit of the Lord shall rest upon him,
>   the Spirit of wisdom and understanding,
>   the Spirit of counsel and might,
>   the Spirit of knowledge and the fear of the Lord.
> [3]And his delight shall be in the fear of the Lord.
> He shall not judge by what his eyes see,
>   or decide disputes by what his ears hear,
> [4]but with righteousness he shall judge the poor,

and decide with equity for the meek of the earth;
and he shall strike the earth with the rod of his mouth,
   and with the breath of his lips he shall kill the wicked.
5Righteousness shall be the belt of his waist,
   and faithfulness the belt of his loins.
6The wolf shall dwell with the lamb,
   and the leopard shall lie down with the young goat,
and the calf and the lion and the fattened calf together;
   and a little child shall lead them.
7The cow and the bear shall graze;
   their young shall lie down together;
   and the lion shall eat straw like the ox.
8The nursing child shall play over the hole of the cobra,
      and the weaned child shall put his hand on the
adder's den.
9They shall not hurt or destroy
   in all my holy mountain;
for the earth shall be full of the knowledge of the Lord
   as the waters cover the sea.

— Isaiah 11:1–9 —

LEADER: The grass withers, the flower fades, but the Word of God remains forever.

GROUP: Amen.

The Singing of a Hymn

In a posture of thankfulness and worship, the Group will then say or sing this hymn together:

Hark! The Herald Angels Sing

Hark! The herald angels sing,
"Glory to the newborn King!"
Peace on earth and mercy mild
God and sinners reconciled
Joyful, all ye nations rise
Join the triumph of the skies
With angelic host proclaim,
"Christ is born in Bethlehem!"

Hark! The herald angels sing,
"Glory to the newborn King!"

Christ, by highest heaven adored
Christ, the everlasting Lord
Late in time, behold Him come
Offspring of the virgin's womb
Veiled in flesh, the Godhead see
Hail the incarnate deity!
Pleased as man with man to dwell
Jesus, our Emmanuel

Hail the heav'n-born Prince of Peace!
Hail the Son of Righteousness!
Light and life to all He brings
Risen with healing in His wings
Born to raise the sons of earth
Born to give them second birth

Scan to sing
hymn with
music and
video.

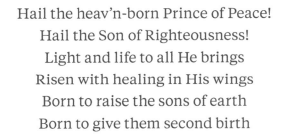

Closing Blessing

The Leader will then close with this prayer:

You, Lord, have become my hope, my comfort, my
strength, my all! In you does my soul rejoice. The
darkness vanished from before my eyes, and I beheld
you, the sun of righteousness. When I loved darkness,
I knew you not, but wandered on from night to night.
But you led me out of that blindness; you took me by the
hand and called me to yourself, and now I can thank
you, and your mighty voice which has penetrated to my
inmost heart. Amen.
— Saint Augustine (354)

The Group will then say the Gloria Patri together:

Glory be to the Father, and to the Son, and to the Holy
Spirit; as it was in the beginning, is now, and will be
forever. Amen.

The Leader will then say:

The grace of the Lord Jesus Christ and the love of God
and the fellowship of the Holy Spirit be with us all.
— 2 Corinthians 13:14

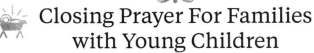

Closing Prayer For Families
with Young Children

Father, thank you for giving us peace through all circumstances in our life. We pray that when we are worried, fearful or afraid we will remember to always seek you first and you will give us peace. Thank you for sending your Son, Jesus, the Prince of Peace to a world that needed him. We love you. Amen

Activities For Families with Young Children

Activity 1:

Draw storm clouds on a piece of construction paper and then write various "storms" that can happen in our lives on each cloud. Then draw a sun and write JESUS GIVES PEACE IN THE MIDDLE OF A STORM. Hang this somewhere in your home that you will all see often.

Activity 2:

As a Family, look up bible verses about peace and write them on strips of paper. Put the bible verse strips in a box. When a member of the Family is feeling anxious, fearful, or worried pull out a verse to remind them where our source of peace comes from. When a bible verse is read, as a Family, memorize the verse about peace.

Application:

Take some time to enjoy fellowship with your Family by baking Christmas cookies and decorating them with the word Peace. Go and offer a plate to your neighbors that day, teachers, and coworkers that week. On Sunday, grab some Christmas Eve Invite cards from your local campus to give out as you do this Family activity.

LOVE

WEEK 3

Opening Blessing

T he Leader may begin by reading one or more of the following. Read slowly, and allow the words to guide your hearts as you begin your time of worship.

Glory to God in the highest, and on earth peace among those with whom he is pleased!

— Luke 2:14 —

"Hear, O Israel: The Lord our God, the Lord is one. You shall love the Lord your God with all your heart and with all your soul and with all your might. And these words that I command you today shall be on your heart.

— Deuteronomy 6:4-6 —

The people who walked in darkness
   have seen a great light;
those who dwelt in a land of deep darkness,
   on them has light shone.
You have multiplied the nation;
   you have increased its joy;
they rejoice before you
   as with joy at the harvest,
   as they are glad when they divide the spoil.

— Isaiah 9:2-3 —

Lighting the Advent Candle

The Leader will go to the Advent table and light the Love candle, the third candle of the Advent wreath. After doing so, the Leader will join the Group and say:

LEADER: The things of this world are passing away.

GROUP: But God's Word remains forever.

LEADER: The world is filled with false love.

GROUP: But God's people see true love in Christ.

LEADER: Hold on to us forever, Lord Jesus.

GROUP: Keep us in Your love, always.

Preparation for Worship and Scripture Reading

The Leader says:

As we approach the throne of our Holy God, we must do so with open hearts. God teaches us that we are not to hide our sins from Him, but rather, we are to confess them freely so as to receive forgiveness and restoration by His grace. Our God is infinitely full of tenderness and love toward us. He never rejects us, despite our many failures. We will approach Him now to confess our sins and prepare our hearts.

The Group will remain silent for 30 seconds while each member privately confesses their sins to God. Families with young children may skip the moment of silence and proceed to the guided prayer, or a parent may lead the children through a personalized prayer.

The Leader will then read this assurance of forgiveness over the Group:

And you, who once were alienated and hostile in mind, doing evil deeds, He has now reconciled in His body of flesh by His death, in order to present you holy and blameless and above reproach before Him, if indeed you continue in the faith, stable and steadfast, not shifting from the hope of the gospel that you heard, which has been proclaimed in all creation under heaven, and of which I, Paul, became a minister.

— Colossians 1:21-23 —

The Leader will then prepare for the reading of Scripture by praying:

Grant, Almighty God, that as you shine on us by your Word, we may not be blind at midday, nor willfully seek darkness, and thus lull our minds asleep; but may we be roused daily by your words, and may we stir up ourselves more and more to fear your name and thus present ourselves and all our pursuits as a sacrifice to you, that you may peaceably rule, and perpetually dwell in us... through Jesus Christ our Lord. Amen.

— John Calvin (1509)

The Leader will take a Bible and say to the Group:

> God's Word is the truth. It is truer than true. It is the greatest treasure we have. In these pages, the Lord Jesus Christ is revealed to us. This home is built upon God's unfailing Word, and our lives are governed by all that He has commanded. Let us never forget this great gift.

The Group will then pray.

LEADER: Oh Lord, we thank You for Your Word.

GROUP: Open our eyes to see You.

LEADER: Father, bless us as we read it.

GROUP: That we may always obey You.

LEADER: Christ, purify us through it.

GROUP: That we may always honor You.

LEADER: Holy Spirit, help us to understand it.

GROUP: That we may always proclaim You.

LEADER: Praise the Lord.

ALL TOGETHER: The Lord's Name be praised.

The Reading of Scripture and Lessons

The Leader will then turn to Genesis 22:1-14. The passage may be read by the Leader or another Group member.

---

¹After these things God tested Abraham and said to him, "Abraham!" And he said, "Here I am." ²He said, "Take your son, your only son Isaac, whom you love, and go to the land of Moriah, and offer him there as a burnt offering on one of the mountains of which I shall tell you." ³So Abraham rose early in the morning, saddled his donkey, and took two of his young men with him, and his son Isaac. And he cut the wood for the burnt offering and arose and went to the place of which God had told him. ⁴On the third day Abraham lifted up his eyes and saw the place from afar. ⁵Then Abraham said to his young men, "Stay here with the donkey; I and the boy will go over there and worship and come again to you." ⁶And Abraham took the wood of the burnt offering and laid it on Isaac his son. And he took in his hand the fire and the knife. So they went both of them together. ⁷And Isaac said to his father Abraham, "My father!" And he said, "Here I am, my son." He said, "Behold, the fire and the wood, but where is the lamb for a burnt offering?" ⁸Abraham said, "God will provide for himself the lamb for a burnt offering, my son." So they went both of them together.

⁹When they came to the place of which God had told him, Abraham built the altar there and laid the wood in order and bound Isaac his son and laid him on the altar, on top of the wood. ¹⁰Then Abraham reached out his hand and took the knife to slaughter his son. ¹¹But the angel of the Lord called to him from heaven and said, "Abraham, Abraham!" And he said, "Here I am." ¹²He said, "Do not lay your hand on the boy or do anything to him, for now I know that you fear God, seeing you have not withheld your son, your only son, from me." ¹³And Abraham lifted up his eyes and looked, and behold, behind him was a ram, caught in a thicket by his horns. And Abraham went and took the ram and offered it up as a burnt offering instead of his son. ¹⁴So Abraham called the name of that place, "The Lord will provide"; as it is said to this day, "On the mount of the Lord it shall be provided."

— Genesis 22:1-14 —

At the end of the reading:

LEADER: This is the Word of the Lord.

GROUP: Thanks be to God.

The Leader will then say:

Today we are reflecting on Jesus Christ, our Love. There is no clearer portrait of God's love than Jesus Christ. What are some of the things you love more than anything else?

The Group will give their answers.

There is no love that quite matches the love between a parent and child. In fact, the first time the word "love" appears in Scripture is here in Genesis 22, referring to Abraham and Isaac. The thought of losing his son would have been unbearable to Abraham. But he had faith that the God of love would provide a lamb for the sacrifice. In faith, he obeyed God's commandment. In this passage, we see God's love in His faithfulness to provide a lamb. Now, in Jesus Christ, the Lamb who takes away our sins, we have the greatest display of God's love.

Let us praise God for the love we have been given in Christ.

Family/Group Scripture Reading

The Leader will then turn to John 3:16-21. This passage may be read by any member of the Group.

[16]"For God so loved the world, that he gave his only Son, that whoever believes in him should not perish but have eternal life. [17]For God did not send his Son into the world to condemn the world, but in order that the world might be saved through him. [18]Whoever believes in him is not condemned, but whoever does not believe is condemned already, because he has not believed in the name of the only Son of God. [19]And this is the judgment: the light has come into the world, and people loved the darkness rather than the light because their works were evil. [20]For everyone who does wicked

things hates the light and does not come to the light, lest his works should be exposed. [21]But whoever does what is true comes to the light, so that it may be clearly seen that his works have been carried out in God."

— John 3:16-21 —

LEADER: The grass withers, the flower fades, but the Word of God remains forever.

GROUP: Amen.

GLORY TO GOD IN THE HIGHEST AND ON EARTH PEACE AMONG THOSE WITH WHOM HE IS PLEASED

— LUKE 2:14 —

The Singing of a Hymn

In a posture of thankfulness and worship, the Group will then say or sing this hymn together:

Sing We The Song Of Emmanuel

Sing we the song of Emmanuel
This the Christ who was long foretold
Lo in the shadows of Bethlehem
Promise of dawn now our eyes behold

God most high in a manger lay
Lift your voices and now proclaim
"Great and glorious, Love has come to us!"
Join now with the host of heaven

Come we to welcome Emmanuel
King who came with no crown or throne
Helpless, He lay, the invincible
Maker of Mary, now Mary's son

O what wisdom to save us all
Shepherds, sages before him fall
Grace and majesty, what humility!
Come on bended knee, adore Him

Scan to sing
hymn with
music and
video.

Go spread the news of Emmanuel
Joy and peace for the weary heart
Lift up your heads for your King has come
Sing for the Light overwhelms the dark

Glory shining for all to see
Hope alive, let the gospel ring
God has made a way! He will have the praise!
Tell the world His name is Jesus

Gloria, gloria
Gloria, gloria

If desired, the Group may sing the additional Hymn,
Come Thou Long Expected Jesus, located in the back of this book.

Closing Blessing

The Leader will then close with these prayers:

> O Lord, who hast mercy upon all, take away from me my sins, and mercifully kindle in me the fire of Thy Holy Spirit. Take away from me the heart of stone, and give me a heart of flesh, a heart to love and adore Thee, a heart to delight in Thee, to follow and enjoy Thee, for Christ's sake.
>> — Saint Ambrose of Milan (400)

> O Sovereign and almighty Lord, bless all Your people, and all Your flock. Give Your peace, Your help, Your love unto us Your servants, the sheep of Your fold, that we may be united in the bond of peace and love, one body and one spirit, in one hope of our calling, in Your divine and boundless love.
>> — Liturgy of Saint Mark (4th century)

The Group will then say the Gloria Patri together:

> Glory be to the Father, and to the Son, and to the Holy Spirit; as it was in the beginning, is now, and will be forever. Amen.

The Leader will then say:

> Now to Him who is able to do far more abundantly than all that we ask or think, according to the power at work within us, to Him be glory in the church and in Christ Jesus throughout all generations, forever and ever. Amen.
>> — Ephesians 3:20-21

Closing Prayer For Families with Young Children

Father, thank you so much for your great love for us. We thank you for sending your one and only Son, Jesus, to save sinners. God, help us to love you more, and to show your love to the people you have placed in our lives. God, we ask these things in your Holy name. Amen.

Activities For Families with Young Children

Activity:

Draw a picture of a heart on a piece of paper for each child. Allow them to decorate and write John 3:16 on their hearts. Once decorated, cut out the heart and tape a loop of string to the top of the heart to make an ornament. Hang the hearts on the Christmas tree for everyone to see as a reminder of God's love for us.

Application:

Take some time to enjoy fellowship by gathering non-perishable food items that your Family can donate to the LifePoint Food Pantry. You can even go ask your neighbors if they have items they would like to donate and explain why your Family is collecting the food. Then grab a box you can put the food in and have the kids decorate the box using whatever festive supplies you have on hand. Then write a personalized prayer for the Family who will receive the box of donated food and stick it in the box.

JOY

WEEK 4

Opening Blessing

The Leader may begin by reading one or more of the following. Read slowly, and allow the words to guide your hearts as you begin your time of worship.

Glory to God in the highest, and on earth peace among those with whom he is pleased!

— Luke 2:14 —

"Hear, O Israel: The Lord our God, the Lord is one. You shall love the Lord your God with all your heart and with all your soul and with all your might. And these words that I command you today shall be on your heart.

— Deuteronomy 6:4-6 —

The people who walked in darkness
   have seen a great light;
those who dwelt in a land of deep darkness,
   on them has light shone.
You have multiplied the nation;
   you have increased its joy;
they rejoice before you
   as with joy at the harvest,
   as they are glad when they divide the spoil.

— Isaiah 9:2-3 —

Lighting the Advent Candle

The Leader will go to the Advent table and light the Joy candle, the fourth candle of the Advent wreath. After doing so, the Leader will join the Group and say:

LEADER: The things of this world are passing away.

GROUP: But God's Word remains forever.

LEADER: The world is filled with sadness and sorrow.

GROUP: But God's people have great joy in Christ.

LEADER: We sing praises to You for You are worthy of praise.

GROUP: Be the joy of our hearts, always.

Preparation for Worship and Scripture Reading

The Leader says:

As we approach the throne of our Holy God, we must do so with open hearts. God teaches us that we are not to hide our sins from Him, but rather, we are to confess them freely so as to receive forgiveness and restoration by His grace. Our God is infinitely full of tenderness and love toward us. He never rejects us, despite our many failures. We will approach Him now to confess our sins and prepare our hearts.

The Group will remain silent for 30 seconds while each member privately confesses their sins to God.

The Leader will then read this assurance of forgiveness over the Group:

but God shows His love for us in that while we were still sinners, Christ died for us. Since, therefore, we have now been justified by His blood, much more shall we be saved by Him from the wrath of God. For if while we were enemies we were reconciled to God by the death of His Son, much more, now that we are reconciled, shall we be saved by His life. More than that, we also rejoice in God through our Lord Jesus Christ, through whom we have now received reconciliation.

— Romans 5:8-11 —

The Leader will then prepare for the reading of Scripture by praying:

Almighty God, and most merciful Father, we humbly submit ourselves, and fall down before your Majesty, asking you from the bottom of our hearts, that this seed of your Word now sown among us, may take such deep root, that neither the burning heat of persecution cause it to wither, nor the thorny cares of this life choke it. But that, as seed sown in good ground, it may bring forth thirty, sixty, or a hundredfold, as your heavenly wisdom has appointed. Amen.

— Middelburg Liturgy (1586)

The Leader will take a Bible and say to the Group:

God's Word is the truth. It is truer than true. It is the greatest treasure we have. In these pages, the Lord Jesus Christ is revealed to us. This home is built upon God's unfailing Word, and our lives are governed by all that He has commanded. Let us never forget this great gift.

The Group will then pray.

LEADER: Oh Lord, we thank You for Your Word.

GROUP: Open our eyes to see You.

LEADER: Father, bless us as we read it.

GROUP: That we may always obey You.

LEADER: Christ, purify us through it.

GROUP: That we may always honor You.

LEADER: Holy Spirit, help us to understand it.

GROUP: That we may always proclaim You.

LEADER: Praise the Lord.

ALL TOGETHER: The Lord's Name be praised.

The Reading of Scripture and Lessons

The Leader will then turn to Luke 1:46-55. The passage may be read by the Leader or another Group member.

⁴⁶ And Mary said,
  "My soul magnifies the Lord,
⁴⁷   and my spirit rejoices in God my Savior,
⁴⁸   for he has looked on the humble estate of his servant.
  For behold, from now on all generations will call me blessed;
⁴⁹   for he who is mighty has done great things for me,
    and holy is his name.
⁵⁰   And his mercy is for those who fear him
    from generation to generation.
⁵¹ He has shown strength with his arm; he has scattered the proud in the thoughts of their hearts;
⁵²   he has brought down the mighty from their thrones
    and exalted those of humble estate;
⁵³   he has filled the hungry with good things,
    and the rich he has sent away empty.
⁵⁴ He has helped his servant Israel,
    in remembrance of his mercy,
⁵⁵ as he spoke to our fathers,
    to Abraham and to his offspring forever."

— Luke 1:46-55 —

At the end of the reading:

> LEADER: This is the Word of the Lord.

> GROUP: Thanks be to God.

The Leader will then say:

> Today we are reflecting on Jesus Christ, our Joy. After all the things she had seen and heard, Mary could not help but sing. Have you ever experienced something so amazing that you wanted to sing about it? Has there ever been a time in your life when you were so overwhelmed with happiness that you had to share it with someone else?

The Group will give their answers.

Deep joy evokes in us a desire to speak, shout, and sing. Mary, along with the rest of her people, had been waiting for thousands of years for the promised Savior to come. Not only had they been waiting, but God had also been silent. No prophets had come with a fresh word from the Lord in 400 years. The people of God may have started to fear that God had abandoned them. But the news that Mary received was the sign that God had a greater word for His people: His Word would take on flesh and dwell among us (John 1:1, 14). This news was worthy of a song. And it is why millions of songs have been written about Jesus since Mary first sang hers.

Let us praise God for the abundant joy we have been given in Christ.

Family/Group Scripture Reading

The Leader will then turn to Psalm 16. This passage may be read by any member of the Group.

[1]Preserve me, O God, for in you I take refuge.
[2]I say to the Lord, "You are my Lord; I have no good apart from you." [3]As for the saints in the land, they are the excellent ones, in whom is all my delight.
[4]The sorrows of those who run after another god shall multiply; their drink offerings of blood I will not pour out or take their names on my lips.
[5]The Lord is my chosen portion and my cup;
    you hold my lot. [6]The lines have fallen for me in pleasant places; indeed, I have a beautiful inheritance.
[7]I bless the Lord who gives me counsel;
    in the night also my heart instructs me.
[8]I have set the Lord always before me;
    because he is at my right hand, I shall not be shaken.
[9]Therefore my heart is glad, and my whole being rejoices; my flesh also dwells secure.
[10]For you will not abandon my soul to Sheol,
    or let your holy one see corruption.
[11]You make known to me the path of life;
    in your presence there is fullness of joy;

— Psalm 16 —

LEADER: The grass withers, the flower fades, but the Word of God remains forever.

GROUP: Amen.

You make
KNOWN TO ME
THE
PATH OF LIFE
In your
PRESENCE
THERE IS
FULLNESS
OF JOY

PSALM 16:11

The Singing of a Hymn

In a posture of thankfulness and worship, the Group will then say or sing this hymn together:

Joy To The World

Joy to the world, the Lord is come
Let earth receive her King
Let every heart prepare Him room
And heaven and nature sing, and heaven and nature sing
And heaven, and heaven and nature sing

Joy to the world, the Savior reigns
Let me their songs employ
While fields and floods, rocks, hills and plains
Repeat the sounding joy, repeat the sounding joy
Repeat, repeat the sounding joy

No more let sins and sorrows grow
Nor thorns infest the ground
He comes to make His blessings flow
Far as the curse is found, far as the curse is found
Far as, far as the curse is found

He rules the world with truth and grace
And makes the nations prove
The glories of His righteousness
And wonders of His love, and wonders of His love
And wonders, wonders of His love

Scan to sing
hymn with
music and
video.

If desired, the Group may sing the additional Hymn,
Angels We Have Heard On High, located in the back of this book.

Closing Blessing

The Leader will then close with this prayer:

Lord, because You have made us, we owe You the whole of our love; Because You have redeemed us, we owe You the whole of ourselves; Because You have promised so much, we owe You our whole being. We owe You much more love than we owe to ourselves, as You are greater than us. We pray You, Lord, make us taste by love what we taste by knowledge; let us know by love what we know by understanding. We owe You more than our whole selves, but we have no more, and by ourselves we cannot render the whole of it to You. Draw us to You, Lord, in the fullness of Your love. We are wholly Yours by creation; make us all Yours, too, in love.

— Saint Anselm (1033)

The Group will then say the Gloria Patri together:

Glory be to the Father, and to the Son, and to the Holy Spirit; as it was in the beginning, is now, and will be forever. Amen.

The Leader will then say:

Now to Him who is able to keep you from stumbling and to present you blameless before the presence of His glory with great joy, to the only God, our Savior, through Jesus Christ our Lord, be glory, majesty, dominion, and authority, before all time and now and forever. Amen.

— Jude 1:24-25

Closing Prayer For Families with Young Children

Jesus, thank you for the joy we have in you. We are thankful for the news of your birth. You are the Messiah. The long awaited one that rescues us from our sin. We praise you for your life, your death, and your resurrection. We pray that we can share the joy of this news to those around us who may not know you. In your name we pray, Amen.

Activities For Families with Young Children

Activity:

Countdown Chain. Cut strips of paper and roll the ends to attach together to make a loop, repeat this step attaching new links to the prior links. Make one loop for each remaining day leading to Christmas. Each morning or night take off the next loop in anticipation of Christmas and the Joy that comes from Jesus being born.

Application:

Take some time to enjoy fellowship by delivering Christmas goodies to your local police station, fire department, or nursing home. Write Christmas Cards that include your favorite Bible verse(s). Pass out Christmas Eve Invite cards as you deliver the goodies.

CHRIST

CHRISTMAS EVE

Opening Blessing

he Leader may begin by reading both of the following passages. Read slowly, and allow the words to guide your hearts as you begin your time of worship.

Glory to God in the highest, and on earth peace among those with whom he is pleased!

— Luke 2:14 —

And the angel said to them, "Fear not, for behold, I bring you good news of great joy that will be for all the people. For unto you is born this day in the city of David a Savior, who is Christ the Lord.

— Luke 2:10-11 —

Lighting the Advent Candle

The Leader will go to the Advent table and light the Christ candle, the fifth candle of the Advent wreath. After doing so, the Leader will join the Group and say:

LEADER: The earth is the Lord's, for He made it.

GROUP: O come, let us adore Him.

LEADER: Worship the Lord in the beauty of holiness.

GROUP: O come, let us adore Him.

LEADER: The mercy of the Lord is everlasting.

GROUP: O come, let us adore Him.

Preparation for Worship and Scripture Reading

The Leader says:

As we approach the throne of our Holy God, we must do so with open hearts. God teaches us that we are not to hide our sins from Him, but rather, we are to confess them freely so as to receive forgiveness and restoration by His grace. Our God is infinitely full of tenderness and love toward us. He never rejects us, despite our many failures. We will approach Him now to confess our sins and prepare our hearts.

The Group will remain silent for 30 seconds while each member privately confesses their sins to God.

The Leader will then read this assurance of forgiveness over the Group:

For God so loved the world, that He gave His only Son, that whoever believes in Him should not perish but have eternal life. For God did not send His Son into the world to condemn the world, but in order that the world might be saved through Him.

— John 3:16-17 —

The Leader will then prepare for the reading of Scripture by praying:

Almighty God, you have given your only-begotten Son to take our nature upon Him, and to be born [this day] of a pure virgin: Grant that we, who have been born again and made your children by adoption and grace, may daily be renewed by your Holy Spirit; through Jesus Christ our Lord, to whom with you and the same Spirit by honor and glory, now and forever. Amen.

— Book of Common Prayer (2019)

The Leader will take a Bible and say to the Group:

God's Word is the truth. It is truer than true. It is the greatest treasure we have. In these pages, the Lord Jesus Christ is revealed to us. This home is built upon God's unfailing Word, and our lives are governed by all that He has commanded. Let us never forget this great gift.

The Group will then pray.

LEADER: Oh Lord, we thank You for Your Word.

GROUP: Open our eyes to see You.

LEADER: Father, bless us as we read it.

GROUP: That we may always obey You.

LEADER: Christ, purify us through it.

GROUP: That we may always honor You.

LEADER: Holy Spirit, help us to understand it.

GROUP: That we may always proclaim You.

LEADER: Praise the Lord.

ALL TOGETHER: The Lord's Name be praised.

The Reading of Scripture and Lessons

The Leader will then turn to Luke 2:8-20. The passage may be read by the Leader, or another Group member.

---

⁸And in the same region there were shepherds out in the field, keeping watch over their flock by night. ⁹And an angel of the Lord appeared to them, and the glory of the Lord shone around them, and they were filled with great fear. ¹⁰And the angel said to them, "Fear not, for behold, I bring you good news of great joy that will be for all the people. ¹¹For unto you is born this day in the city of David a Savior, who is Christ the Lord. ¹²And this will be a sign for you: you will find a baby wrapped in swaddling cloths and lying in a manger." ¹³And suddenly there was with the angel a multitude of the heavenly host praising God and saying,

¹⁴"Glory to God in the highest, and on earth peace among those with whom he is pleased!"

¹⁵When the angels went away from them into heaven, the shepherds said to one another, "Let us go over to Bethlehem and see this thing that has happened, which the Lord has made known to us." ¹⁶And they went with haste and found Mary and Joseph, and the baby lying in a manger. ¹⁷And when they saw it, they made known the saying that had been told them concerning

this child. ¹⁸And all who heard it wondered at what the shepherds told them. ¹⁹But Mary treasured up all these things, pondering them in her heart. ²⁰And the shepherds returned, glorifying and praising God for all they had heard and seen, as it had been told them.

— Luke 2:8-20 —

LEADER: This is the Word of the Lord.

GROUP: Thanks be to God.

The Leader will then say:

Christ is the One who makes Christmas special. The good news is that after all the gifts have been opened, the parties have ended, and the food has been eaten, Christ will remain. Christ, the King of Glory, entered the world He created to bring hope, peace, love, and joy. How rich a treasure we possess in Jesus Christ, our Lord! How immeasurable is His greatness and how wonderful is His love! Forever we will praise Him, our Immanuel, our God incarnate, our Savior and King.

LEADER: The grass withers, the flower fades, but the Word of God remains forever.

GROUP: Amen.

The Singing of a Hymn

In a posture of thankfulness and worship, the Group will then say or sing this hymn together:

Hark! The Herald Angels Sing

O holy night, the stars are brightly shining
It is the night of our dear Savior's birth
Long lay the world in sin and error pining
'Til He appeared and the soul felt its worth
A thrill of hope, the weary world rejoices
For yonder breaks a new and glorious morn

Fall on your knees
Oh hear the angel voices
Oh night divine, oh night when Christ was born
Oh night divine, oh night divine

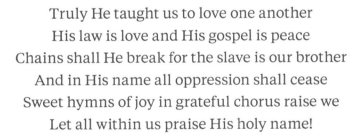

Scan to sing
hymn with
music and
video.

Truly He taught us to love one another
His law is love and His gospel is peace
Chains shall He break for the slave is our brother
And in His name all oppression shall cease
Sweet hymns of joy in grateful chorus raise we
Let all within us praise His holy name!

Christ is the Lord
Oh praise His name forever
His power and glory evermore proclaim
His power and glory evermore proclaim

If desired, the Group may sing the additional Hymn,
Come Thou Long Expected Jesus, located in the back of this book.

Closing Blessing

The Leader will then close with this prayer:

> Christ with me, Christ before me,
> Christ behind me,
> Christ in me, Christ beneath me,
> Christ above me,
> Christ on my right, Christ on my left,
> Christ when I lie down, Christ when I sit,
> Christ when I stand,
> Christ in the heart of everyone who thinks of me,
> Christ in the mouth of everyone who speaks of me,
> Christ in every eye that sees me,
> Christ in every ear that hears me.
> — Saint Patrick (387)

The Leader will say:

> The kingdom of the world has become the kingdom of our Lord and of his Christ, and he shall reign forever and ever.
> — Revelation 11:15

The Group will then say together:

> Glory be to the Father, and to the Son, and to the Holy Spirit; as it was in the beginning, is now, and will be forever. Amen.

Final Christmas Blessing

Members of the Group will each say one of these lines to the rest of the Group. If there are more lines than Group members, someone may say more than one.

May you know the joy of Jesus, and may the joy of Jesus be with you.

May you know the peace of our God, and may the peace of our God be with you.

May you know the hope of the Spirit, and may the hope of the Spirit be with you.

May you know the love of our Lord, and may the love of our Lord be with you.

LEADER: Christ the Lord will reign forever.
GROUP: Forever He will reign.

The Leader will then say:

Now to him who is able to strengthen you according to my gospel and the preaching of Jesus Christ, according to the revelation of the mystery that was kept secret for long ages but has now been disclosed and through the prophetic writings has been made known to all nations, according to the command of the eternal God, to bring about the obedience of faith—to the only wise God be glory forevermore through Jesus Christ! Amen.
— Romans 16:25-27

Closing Prayer For Families with Young Children

God, today we are reminded and incredibly thankful for the gift of your Son. Thank you for your plan to rescue us and bring us into right relationship with you. Do not allow us to make Christmas about anything else other than your Son. Father, we pray for those that do not know this truth today. May we be bold enough to proclaim you to those who do not know you in the way we live our life and the way we interact with them.

Activities For Families with Young Children

Activity:

Gather as a Family around the Bible and read Luke 2:1-20 together. Take time to focus on the real meaning and truth of Christmas. Give each Family member a journal or something to write on. List out reasons you are thankful for Jesus. List out truths that we have because of His birth, His life, His death, His resurrection. Talk about these things as a Family.

Application:

Prepare a passage of Scripture that one of the children can read to the entire Family during Christmas dinner. If the child is too young to read, coach them so that they can give a sentence or two about the meaning of Christmas to share with the Family.

Christmas Morning

Join us online for a short Christmas program as we celebrate the birth of Jesus.

Find the video at lifept.org or the LifePoint Church App. Scan the code below to view the video.

The Upcoming Year

Our prayer is that the Family/Group worship guides, daily Advent meditations, and activities in this book have been a great encouragement to you during this season of worship and reflection on the incarnation of the Lord Jesus Christ. We want to end by pointing you toward reading plans where you will continue engaging with the Scriptures and enjoying the Lord Jesus in the coming year.

Discover bible reading plans on our website at lifept.org/bible. Scan the code below to visit the webpage.

Additional Hymns

Come Thou Long Expected Jesus

Come Thou long expected Jesus
Born to set Thy people free
From our fears and sins release us
Let us find our rest in Thee

Israel's strength and consolation
Hope of all the earth Thou art
Dear desire of every nation
Joy of every longing heart

Born Thy people to deliver
Born a child, and yet a King
Born to reign in us forever
Now Thy gracious kingdom bring

By Thine own eternal Spirit
Rule in all our hearts alone
By Thine all-sufficient merit
Raise us to Thy glorious throne

Scan to sing
hymn with
music and
video.

BORN

TO SET *Thy*

PEOPLE

FREE

Hark The Herald Angels Sing

(Charles Wesley, 1739)[a]

Hark! The herald angels sing,
"Glory to the newborn King!"
Peach on earth and mercy mild
God and sinners reconciled
Joyful, all ye nations rise
Join the triumph of the skies
With angelic host proclaim,
"Christ is born in Bethlehem!"

Hark! The herald angels sing,
"Glory to the newborn King!"

Christ, by highest heaven adored
Christ, the everlasting Lord
Late in time, behold Him come
Offspring of the virgin's womb
Veiled in flesh, the Godhead see
Hail the incarnate deity!
Pleased as man with man to dwell
Jesus, our Emmanuel

Hail the heav'n-born Prince of Peace!
Hail the Son of Righteousness!
Light and life to all He brings
Risen with healing in His wings
Born to raise the sons of earth
Born to give them second birth

Scan to sing
hymn with
music and
video.

Go Tell It On the Mountain

While shepherds kept their watching
O'er silent flocks by night
Behold, throughout the heavens
There shone a holy light

Go tell it on the mountain,
Over the hills and everywhere;
Go tell it on the mountain
That Jesus Christ is born!

The shepherds feared and trembled
When lo, above the earth
Rang out the angel chorus
That hailed our Savior's birth

Down in a lowly manger
Our humble Christ was born
And God sent us salvation
That blessed Christmas morn

Scan to sing
hymn with
music and
video.

Sing We The Song Of Emmanuel

Sing we the song of Emmanuel
This the Christ who was long foretold
Lo in the shadows of Bethlehem
Promise of dawn now our eyes behold

God most high in a manger lay
Lift your voices and now proclaim
"Great and glorious, Love has come to us!"
Join now with the host of heaven

Come we to welcome Emmanuel
King who came with no crown or throne
Helpless, He lay, the invincible
Maker of Mary, now Mary's son

O what wisdom to save us all
Shepherds, sages before him fall
Grace and majesty, what humility!
Come on bended knee, adore Him

Go spread the news of Emmanuel
Joy and peace for the weary heart
Lift up your heads for your King has come
Sing for the Light overwhelms the dark

Glory shining for all to see
Hope alive, let the gospel ring
God has made a way! He will have the praise!
Tell the world His name is Jesus

Gloria, gloria
Gloria, gloria

I Heard The Bells

I heard the bells on Christmas Day
Their old, familiar carols play
And wild and sweet the words repeat
Of peace on earth, goodwill to men.

'Til ringing, singing on it's way
The world revolved from night to day
A voice, a chime, a chant sublime
Of peace on earth, goodwill to men.

And in despair I bowed my head
"There is no peace on earth" I said,
For hate is strong and mocks the song
Of peace on earth, goodwill to men.

Then pealed more loud and deep
God is not dead, nor doth He sleep
The wrong shall fail, the right prevail
With peace on earth, goodwill to men.

Peace on earth, goodwill to men!
Peace on earth, goodwill to men!

Scan to sing
hymn with
music and
video.

Joy To The World

Joy to the world, the Lord is come
Let earth receive her King
Let every heart prepare Him room
And heaven and nature sing, and heaven and nature sing
And heaven, and heaven and nature sing

Joy to the world, the Savior reigns
Let me their songs employ
While fields and floods, rocks, hills and plains
Repeat the sounding joy, repeat the sounding joy
Repeat, repeat the sounding joy

No more let sins and sorrows grow
Nor thorns infest the ground
He comes to make His blessings flow
Far as the curse is found, far as the curse is found
Far as, far as the curse is found

He rules the world with truth and grace
And makes the nations prove
The glories of His righteousness
And wonders of His love, and wonders of His love
And wonders, wonders of His love

Scan to sing
hymn with
music and
video.

O Come All Ye Faithful (We Adore Thee)

O come, all ye faithful
Joyful and triumphant
O come ye, o come ye to Bethlehem
Come and behold Him
Born the King of angels

O come, let us adore Him
O come, let us adore Him
O come, let us adore Him
Christ the Lord

Sing, choirs of angels, sing in exultation
Sing, all ye citizens of heaven above
Glory to God, all glory in the highest

How we adore Thee, how we adore Thee
Righteous and holy, our Savior
True God from true God, Light everlasting
Jesus, we love Thee, Christ the Lord!

Yea, Lord we greet Thee, born this happy morning
Jesus, to Thee be all glory giv'n
Word of the Father, no in flesh appearing

Scan to sing
hymn with
music and
video.

O Holy Night

O holy night, the stars are brightly shining
It is the night of our dear Savior's birth
Long lay the world in sin and error pining
'Til He appeared and the soul felt its worth
A thrill of hope, the weary world rejoices
For yonder breaks a new and glorious morn

Fall on your knees
Oh hear the angel voices
Oh night divine, oh night when Christ was born
Oh night divine, oh night divine

Truly He taught us to love one another
His law is love and His gospel is peace
Chains shall He break for the slave is our brother
And in His name all oppression shall cease
Sweet hymns of joy in grateful chorus raise we
Let all within us praise His holy name!

Christ is the Lord
Oh praise His name forever
His power and glory evermore proclaim
His power and glory evermore proclaim

Scan to sing
hymn with
music and
video.

Angels We Have Heard On High

Angels we have heard on high
Sweetly singing o'er the plains
And the mountains in reply
Echoing their joyous strains

Gloria in excelsis Deo
Gloria in excelsis Deo

Shepherds, why this jubilee?
Why your joyous strains prolong?
What the gladsome tidings be
Which inspire your heavenly song?

Come to Bethlehem and see
Him whose birth the angels sing
Come, adore on bended knee
Christ the Lord, the newborn King

See Him in a manger laid
Jesus, Lord of heaven and earth
Mary, Joseph lend your aid
With us sing our Savior's birth

Scan to sing
hymn with
music and
video.

HEAVENLY
HOSTS SING
ALLELUIA
Christ THE
SAVIOR IS
BORN

Silent Night

Silent night, holy night
All is calm, all is bright
'Round yon virgin, mother and child
Holy infant so tender and mild
Sleep in heavenly peace
Sleep in heavenly peace

Silent night, holy night
Shepherds quake at the sight
Glories stream from heaven afar
Heavenly hosts sing "Alleluia!"
Christ the Savior is born!
Christ the Savior is born!

Silent night, holy night
Son of God, love's pure light
Radiant beams from Thy holy face
With the dawn of redeeming grace
Jesus, Lord at Thy birth!
Jesus, Lord at Thy birth!

Scan to sing
hymn with
music and
video.

CPSIA information can be obtained
at www.ICGtesting.com
Printed in the USA
LVHW070044081122
732334LV00001B/1

9 781088 064450